PATRIARCHY BLUES

RENA PRIEST

PATRIARCHY BLUES

POEMS

MoonPathPress

Poetry
ISBN 978-1-936657-27-8

Cover art: photograph by Sarah Katharina Kayss
http://www.sarahkatharinakayss.com/

Author photo: by Lela Childs

Design by Tonya Namura
using Liquiorstore Jazz and Gill Sans

MoonPath Press is dedicated to publishing the finest poets
of the U.S. Pacific Northwest

MoonPath Press
PO Box 445
Tillamook, OR 97141

MoonPathPress@gmail.com

http://MoonPathPress.com

*This collection is dedicated
to the subterranean
homesick matriarchy*

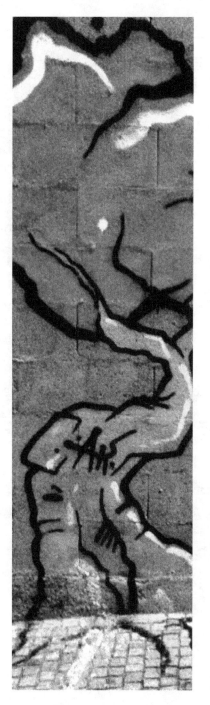

"I merely took the energy
it takes to pout and
wrote some blues."
—Duke Ellington

Contents

PATRIARCHY BLUES

Toward a Beautiful Flare of Ruin

Is safety crippling? Better to be a fierce,
and hungry, and angry thing of tastes,
and moods, and tempers; to devour?

To long for achingly? To walk in between?
To hide from oneself? To hide from others?
To indulge and set free, and destroy?

To wish harm on and take it back?
To wish not to wish harm on. To howl
and wander, shameless of the appetites

and the failure to desire to curb them.
To follow the cravings illicitly. To follow,
knowing where they lead.

Or, to turn the desires away and open
the heart to fall prey to hunger, and lack,
and jealousy, and shame, and meanness?

To lose touch with the fluidity of the spirit?
To find new desires and cultivate tastes for
the sunrise? To trade the sweetness of

transient pleasures for the steady sweetness
of your own voice. To be destroyed,
and rebuilt by songs.

Desire is a Scissor

Desire is a scissor,
searching for us at the ends
of loose threads, tugged,
unraveling into a luster,
a bliss faced blush
across 17 muscles to smile
and 43 muscles to frown.

Unraveled into a dazzle,
a tuft of down
swirling from the apex
where none can plant their flag.
It holds us;
this shine muck, electric fence.
We hold it for the jolt and throb
of fingers buzzing in our blood,
the spool unwound, bound
up in new seams.

We find we can't let go.
Even for life.
It is a parallel striped longing
leading off into the distance;
so far off that the two lines
seem to join at the horizon,
but never really do.

They just stay,
the exact same distance apart.

It is the un-navigable
distance of want.

What does it mean, little guru?
This lopsided enlightenment,
the night's firmament collapsing
into a single, hot moment,
does it dull your senses forever?

Kitchen Tools, Sometimes Wire Cutters
After DFW

Despite the grotesquerie
of lush clichés, we all
seem to watch, though,
there's no more real joy
about it. We all pretend
there's joy; pretending not to know
the whole thing sucks.
[Laughter, cheers, ovation.]
I'm going to hell. But that's
okay, 'cause all my friends'll
be there too. [applause.]
Every time I find a gray hair
I fuck my wife, (the woman
I'm astounded with)
like a depraved pantomime,
laughing uproariously
during a routine climax,
(all the clichés are true.)
The whole irony-free zone,
(famous for stardust on neon
with its big mirage; its huge,
intricate, towering, smoking hue;
a museum of spectacle,
fake conqueror of its own
empire of self,)
It's breathtaking! Makes
all the neon bleed,

too pretty to stand. Everyone,
without exception,
is sweating.

Dear Mr. Shaffer,

If I had the right kind of laser,
and you had an electron microscope,
I could write secret love letters to you
in the curve of a paperclip.
They might be short, little verses
about the abundant nature of love.
The paper clip might be holding together
a movie script about the apocalypse,
and scarcity. Maybe, when you pulled the
message-encoded paperclip from the script,
every page would tumble away
to be edited by wear and rough weather,
so that only the sweetest lines were legible.
Only the words "you," and "enough,"
and "you-are-always-enough,"
so that weeks later, when strangers
on train platforms picked up the scraps
gusted into their hair, they might feel as if
they were getting love letters from the wind.

Van der Waal's Force

You take my hand,
look at my fingerprints,
and ask, "Did I ever tell you how
a gecko sticks to the ceiling?"

You explain how gecko toes
have grooves
that turn into a forest of hairs,
which have smaller sub-hairs
with a forest of smaller
sub-hairs, and so on,
until at the very tips
are atoms.

So, the gecko toe
and the ceiling atoms
are joined,
become one.
Momentarily—
indistinguishable.

"And it's so freaky cool,"
you say.
"The military has studied it.
They've tried,
but they can't manufacture
anything like that."

Mantrum

*"She's gone. I am abused, and my relief must be to
loathe her."* —Othello

You are gone.
Gone.

I am alone.
Alone.

I have gone to work
on an operating system
for a flying death machine.

The military is paying me handsomely,
though,
I don't know what to do with the money.
You are gone.

There are a bunch of people here,
who I went to high school with,
who I don't like.
I never did.

I'm afraid I'm going to die.
I'm not sure why, but
that's the tenor of the situation.

Vinegar

It's midnight.
The neighbors are fighting again.
There is the sound of something precious
breaking.

A door slams,
then weeping.

A memory of good days
caught in the jam, smarts,
bleeds room temperature tears,
throbs blue, goes numb.

The huckleberry door,
the color of a bruise,
is the loneliest sight.
He escapes through it,

finds no way but back to her,
to shared solitude;
the forgiving arms of need.
His hand curls

into a pleading fist.
He swallows vinegar and knocks.
It's midnight.
The neighbors are fighting again.

There is the sound
of something precious breaking.
A door slams,
then weeping.

Billboard Dream Girl's Waking Life

"I want to smash your pretty little face."
"You think I'm pretty?" This banter,
brutal and tender; a prelude?

I have been told that dreams
are the training grounds for
difficult situations: Our true love leaving us;

the world suddenly, unexpectedly morphing
into something we don't understand;
things or people changing

into other things or people. Dreams
are where we practice for the passage of time.
In the unhappiest of passages

there is a promise. A terrifying promise,
that says you need to ruin yourself again.
This building—this life, is not

the correct version. It's all wrong.
You will tear it down and wander the streets
tattered and insane. Let people show disdain.

Take their pictures and make an ad. Disdain
is the sexy-face that sells a zillion push-up bras.
The Victoria's Secret ad men know

how guys ache to give it to a bitchy-faced gal,
how they crave that sexy, savage snarl
on perfectly symmetrical, delicate features,

suggesting this beautiful creature
is thinking, *I want to murder you, motherfucker,*
but you are much more powerful than I.

Now you tell me, what is sexier than that?
Just picture her: suggestive pose, hair blown back,
that look on her face… the stuff of fantasy, no?

The brain is the same brain when it's dreaming
as it is when it's awake. It's the same world.
The same reality. The very same.

Live Nude Girl's Favorite Thing to Feel

All night, men reach up
to touch her ankles.
Mornings, on her stoop
she smokes, while
the neighbor kid asks
about all her favorite things.

"What's your favorite
thing to feel?" he asks,
holding up his softest
blanket, giving it a rub
between his finger
and his thumb.

She wants to tell him
her favorite thing
to feel is love,
but keeps coming back
to the secret she
discovered a week ago.

Waking in the night,
her left arm, dead asleep,
was a limb of luscious flesh,
foreign and remote. She used
her working hand to lift it
and rest it on her chest.

The sensational feeling
of her own sensationless skin

surprised her. Startled,
she thought of Narcissus,
swallowed up, drowned
in his own sweetness. Lost.

So soft, so soft. She never knew,
never understood all those
desperate reaching hands.

Lament for the Love of Bunny

She can eat a man whole with her eyes—
lick his skinny bones white, sweat him
from her pores in the fever

of a cold, cold night.
It would have the smell of stargazer lilies, wilting,
and the whole thing would sound like a soft sigh.

When first I saw her, she had big hair
and a blacked eye. She said, "I could make
loving you my business. That would be a good

first line." But she's closed up shop
and there will be no more sighing like that
on our block. She took the red light down.

Left us to remember the washed out stars
above her lonely stoop and a panatela's hot display.
These days, we smoke and the time just goes,

while our sons of these concrete gardens
grow, gray, but hard—blossom into stone.
Did I ever tell you how once after lovemaking,

Bunny saw a roach the size of a meadow lark
crawling into the sunlight to die?
She would see an ugly thing and sing,

"I wanna be a part of it. New York, New York!"
but she's gone—took the girls uptown.
Bought them all a home—learned to sew.

At least I don't love her no more.
So how could we be low, beneath these bright lights,
though Bunny took the red one down?

When You Are Blue

I slap your lovely face and laugh
and slap your face again, then
shake your name into your chest.

I kiss your purple slanted lips,
and slap your lovely face again.
You are still and blue, like 4 a.m.

We've been through this before.
I know the limits of true love's kiss,
so I slap your lovely face some more.

You gasp and murmur,
"Stop hitting me." Your cheeks
now pink with sting,

I sigh and say,
"Oh, Sweetheart,
for blueness it's the only thing."

Pink Frosted Cake

A phone rings, unanswered, in another apartment.
A car alarm rings, neglected, in the street
Your watch beeps and you say, "Oh, I think
I should go back on anti-depressants.
It's always the same-
old grind; and then,
there's all the world's tragedy."

"Why all the sad songs?"
I ask, trying to reassure you
that you're wrong.
Acquiescing into the gray morning,
you say at 4 a.m., "I got no reason
to get up today." And we laugh, because
since we found each other, it just means

having a day off from work,
instead of having no reason to live.
"Do you think there's a difference
between things existing
and not existing?"
I ask, to meld a bond.
You don't care.

It's been 127 hours
since you've had a cigarette,
and you claim you can't go on
without my getting naked
and putting on that pink chiffon apron
so I can bake you a cake that says,

"You are the King!" And I would,
if only you'd quit telling me
how I don't love you anymore.
My darling, my sugar coma,
wouldn't you like to stop all this nonsense
and let me read to you
from the diary of every kiss?

Faithful

Every day she prays: "Lord, please
let me leave that man alone."

Often she means the deli worker,
with graceful, meaty hands
who looks as if he's imagining
her climax face as she tells him
how much salami she needs.

Sometimes "that man"
is the contractor
renovating her kitchen.
She imagines the white smudges
of his fingers on her body,
and how she'd fit in his angles,
like a glistening blush
of pink insulation.

Alone, in her apron,
she is the Betty Crocker
of suffering and refrain.
In her dishpan hands
sweetness denied,
affection withheld,
disappointments, bitter
as baker's chocolate,
become decadent.

She turns it all to devil's food,
while she harmonizes

with her appliances
in the wistful song of sighs,
that is the music of breakfast,
lunch, and supper. The dirge
of a faithful, household angel.

Nail Salon

The colors shimmer
in rows along the walls,
like springtime on shrooms.
A conundrum conjuring variety,
glistening like an impossible city.
Choice is always a factor
in happiness.
The more choices we're given,
the greater our capacity
for dissatisfaction.
It's okay. There's always red,
but then, there they stand
a selection sorted aside; sordid
in their suggestion. "Snake's tongue!"
Granny used to call painted nails.
"Poesis!" I say. The name
to make the shade.
"Fishnet Stockings," red.
"Freaky Friday Night," red.
"Gypsy Girl," red.
"Vodka and Caviar," red.
"Drive Church Ladies Insane
With Envy," red.
"Cat Fight," red.
"Will Somebody Please Pay
Attention to ME?!" red.
All this and still, I can't find
a shade to fit the statement that
I want to make:
"This Predatory, Capitalist, Patriarchy

is Killing Me and I'm Trying
to Learn to Like It." Why
have I never seen that shade in here before?
Probably, the labels are too small
so they call it, "Girl,
Just Gamboge and Forget It."

Creeping Out of Orbit

"For what is virtue but the lack of strong temptation?"
—Stephen Dobyns

Standing on her shadow in the sunshine
she says, "I hear the moon is a woman.
I'll bet she'd like to turn her shining face
toward darker, freer, secret places." Once,
she went to pick you up and on your bed
was an antique open lexicon.
The first word on the page she read
was one she'd never seen before
and can't remember, anymore.
It was a verb that meant to bend
toward moonlight. And that's how it was.
How she bent toward your bed
and that solid word on a diaphanous
page. It hooked her tongue with serifs
and burdened her rest, as she tried to recall
the feel of it in her mouth, in the moonlight,
where she feels her meaning slip like neon
from a cracked sign. Bending,
she imagines the creak before the snap.
Is desire not acted upon a betrayal?

Mrs.

In a quiet window, contemplating
the length of a million years,
I watch the snowfall.

You come sit next to me, and ask
if I've changed my name. "Oh, I suppose,"
I say. You ask if I associate

the tradition of a woman taking
her husband's name with slavery.
"Oh, I suppose," I say.

We smile at each other, and I ask,
"How far back do you suppose
I'd have to go,

to get a woman's name?"
You shrug and look out the window.
Between us the sound of snow

accumulates, while we consider
names and marriage,
and lengthy stretches of time.

Desire at the Stitch and Bitch

Your name makes a sound
like a dropped spool
bouncing on a sunlit floor.

Gwendolyn, Gwendolyn.

I repeat it to myself while I sew.
Lost in it, my needle surprises me,
emerging from the seersucker sleeve in my lap.

Whose hands are these? I am losing buttons.

I have seen you looking at me,
as if you know it's me
who's been sending the prayers

from the prayer wheels in your shrine;

carving lurid desires in their stead.
Desires unraveling my nights while I spin in my bed,
desires saving the world from sickness and death

sickness and death which exist less and less,

now that all day my eyes eat shine, and my body
is nourished by drums and bells, and my soul
—what else tastes to it

like something unrequited?

Yet, I have seen you over there
looking at me—up from your embroidery
every now and then, a glance

and your hands forget the thread.

The Rental Dog

The train came and the man
sat next to me, showed me
a photo of his daughter, told me
the story of his life. "Kicked out!"

he said, of the German air-force,
his marriage, his home. He
had just returned from New Mexico…
"I was out there living in a teepee,

trying to get clean of the New York guck."
He paused,
"My rental dog was eaten by coyotes.
They lured him with a female in heat.

They're cannibals you know."
The dog's true owner was a hippie girl.
She took the news like business.
"It's nature, stupid dog," was all she said.

Later, I told his story to an optimist
named Nancy. She believes:
"The dog *ran away* with the coyotes.
Shrugged off his rental dog existence;

became a real dog, baying at the moon."
But looking at this man, I remembered
hearing that a pet takes on
the characteristics of its companion,

and Nancy's theory seems implausible,
for this man has in his eyes the look
of a rental dog, unloved, and therefore,
easily lured and devoured.

Pruning the Wilderness

There is no great tragedy awaiting me.
Yet, something keeps pulling me back
toward humility.

Desire is a trap I keep falling into,
like dire wolves into a tar pit
thinking, *What luck! Look at the*
mammoth just standing there,
crying in the drinking hole.

Nothing is ever that easy.
Nature makes you pay
for wanting something easy.
The trick, you see, is
you have to conquer your mind.

Satisfaction

They are kissing
and talking in the tones
of lovers. Hunger hums
at the edges of their words,
softened and warm, rising
in clouds around the engines
of their heads. I advance
toward their bench.
The man looks up.
The woman looks away.
I lower my eyes and
continue beyond them,
deep into the lonely park,
where I see a pigeon
pulling a chicken-leg
from the mesh of a trash can
beside an empty bench,
where I sit to rest,
while the pigeon,
in the lamplight,
plucks strings of meat
from bone.
He looks as if he's kissing it
gently, while in his throat,
is the warm sound
of satisfied lovers.

The Encyclopedia Britannica, Sunshine, A Mosquito

Strays, with the blood of 100,000 stick people.
The confetti is a wilted sickness; pox
against glittering sunshine in puddles.

Can you climb into a person's
longing for you and float away?

You can wear balloons in your hair,
instead of roses.

Can you make a hen forge checks
with her chicken scratch?
Can you put her egg under a down pillow
and see if it hatches into a smaller, down pillow—
a decorative pillow?

You can write "I love you," in the dirt
if you have a sharp enough hatchet.

A bunch of pens, two songs and a heartbreak
will easily fit into a quart berry-basket.

Would you eat paper covered in mental illness
and secrets?

Could you breathe rainclouds?
Could you breathe lightning from the lungs
behind your lungs?

If I were shrunk down to the size of a pea,
I would do regular-sized crossword-puzzles
with a miniature pen. It would be my daily workout.

If I had a tail, I would use it to make gestures
so everyone would know
when I was becoming agitated.

The Hobo and His Pigeons

The sound-the-sound of longing in the streets,
Ti-tum-ti-tum-ti-tum-ti-tum-ti-tum.
My chum's a bum for rum who lives in slums.
He craves the meat of beasts with beets and leeks,
and sings his longing to the burdened beaks
of birds who sing, "I want, I want, ti-tum."
Those burdened beaks, they long and sing for crumb
from bum with rum and roses in his cheeks.

And when he speaks he coos them out a jest
of bars and men and broads and roads he's known
to give them ease of heavy, hungry loads
and fill their beaks with sweetened emptiness,
while he forgets the bleary, blurry cold
in songs of longing and remembrances.

Window Dressings

Saks 5th Ave., I walk past it every day.
The chalk-fair mannequins
make me afraid, with their sharp
elbows and hard frames,
posed so imposingly, so mean
just like frigid rich white women,
standing guard in the windows
over treasures meant only
for frigid rich white women.

Next door is St. Patrick's
passing no judgments,
reminding me to do the same.
And on the street out front,
is the summer home
of a handsome, homeless man
with a tied up bed roll, and two cats
trained to play dead when he takes aim
with his finger and his thumb,
and fires his imaginary gun.

I've also seen him in a lotus pose
outside the Armani Exchange,
where in the windows today,
a dozen live greased up men;
are shimmering, shaved,
and tanning-booth-toasted all over;
mostly naked in their tighty whities.
Undressed to sell expensive clothes,
they flex and pull faces

at a bombardment of photo flashes
that bounce from their skin, teeth,
and hair like sparks from wasted
bullets, invincible as the mythology
of success, the fantasy of power.

"This is what it looks like. This
is what you want to look like."

Later, each superman
puts back on his own clothes,
and returns home along the same,
reeking streets as the rest of us.

He will eat his dinner
and only feel the creep of his frailty,
tugging once or twice.

Commentary at the Precipice

It teeters.

    Spectators remark on their nerves,
    how like crickets
    exuding the uncertainty of dawn
    they chirp friction songs asking, *still night?*
    still night?
    is it, still night?
    waiting to fall silent beneath
    the grand parade of light.

        "And who are you?" comes a voice.

Meantime, we stand on the sugar line,
waiting for our turn to die.
Open yourself to it.
We each think we have something pure
until we taste it.
There is no shame in liking it.

        Head long, head, more head,
        broadly, brink, steadies itself,
        still, a very steep or
      overhanging place—
        a hazardous situation, like
        traveling in a limousine
        across an ice covered lake,
        drinking vodka from the bottle
        while a lover cries along
        the ice-stacked banks.

There is a child awake at 2 a.m.
Why is that child awake?
On a stoop a drunkard listens
to the crying of the child,
and taunts a deadly spider,
throwing bug sized bits of grass
into its web beneath the stair.
The stars should be mentioned here.

The crime rate has fallen,
    it has been proposed,
    not because of gun control,
    but because of a decision for Roe.
    The unwanted people
have all been taken care of and so,
    do not have to take
    from the rest of us to fill the hole
    where love was supposed to go.
    And would-be-parents
    do not have to do more than one
    unforgivable thing
    to their child.

        The granules are rough. The sugar is bright.

A well-mannered lady loves topiary—
cultivation, loveliness,
the relationship between suffering
and the artificial shaping
of a naturally beautiful thing.

Cutting should be mentioned here.
　　Man-made perfection, except where
　　an unexpected freeze
　　opens a hole in the leafy down,
　　revealing a skeletal tangle,
　　a network of emptiness
　　holding bits of light.

Return. The bone-marked sluice is dry and now where?
Where is all that exhaust-stained snow we thought would
never melt?
And those oil-slick puddles we thought would never dry?

They have receded, and we see there
the ribcage of a deer, and a smaller ribcage beside.

Past a certain hour
the sound of crickets becomes
the sound of a minds friction;
flint casting sparks,
catching nothing,
disappearing in the dark.

There is no hour past which
the sugar mill does not grind
the smell of refinement into the sky—
all but whiteness
and sweetness
burned away.

The Perils of Flight

The scenario is this: A bird is stuck in the house,
much like you have seen many times as a child.
Your hands keep reaching for the flutter of wings
and withdrawing as the bird protests. You know
if it cannot be retrieved, the bird will die.

Quiet Children

I notice how bees keep flying
to the emptiness in the tree
where their home used to be.
They don't disturb the children
playing in my driveway, oblivious
to the hovering above their ears.

I watch them from my steps
and listen to the green collision
of a million leaves, unsettled by a breeze.
A car staggers by, dragging along
a swarm of summer dust.
The children have all gone quiet.

They are in a circle, wiggling
and whispering about something
on the ground. I investigate, and see
a wrecked hive, the color of winter.
The older boys, in their cruelty
were at it last night with stones.

I shoo the children away, tell them,
"Go play." The doomed larvae strive
and vibrate. I cringe, but can't help
looking and looking, even days later,
at those starving conic bodies,
shimmering in their pale hexagon cells.

Acknowledgments

"Toward a Beautiful Flare of Ruin," title taken from a passage in Donna Tartt's book, *The Goldfinch*.

"Desire is a Scissor," first appeared as a featured work at the Anchor Art Space in, "Strands: Draw, Cut Stitch, Write," a collaborative exhibition of poetry and visual arts.

"Kitchen Tools, Sometimes Wire Cutters," is an erasure of David Foster Wallace's essay, *Big Red Son*.

"Desire at the Stitch and Bitch," first appeared in *Stirring: A Literary Collection*.

"Lament for the Love of Bunny," first appeared in *Diagram*.

"Live Nude Girl's Favorite Thing to Feel," first appeared in *Noisy Water: Poetry from Whatcom County, Washington*.

"The Hobo and His Pigeons" is forthcoming in the World Enough Writers: *Beer, Wine, & Spirits Anthology*.

About the Author

Rena Priest is a writer, poet, and concerned citizen. She is a Lummi tribal member and was raised in a subterranean homesick matriarchy. She holds an MFA from Sarah Lawrence College, and is active in efforts to strengthen community through participation in local arts and culture.